BREVILLE SMART AIR FRYER OVEN COOKBOOK

50 Wholesome Crispy And Delicious Recipes
For Healthy Eating, From Breakfast To
Dinner, For Beginners And Advanced Users

Ashley Coleman

Table of Contents

INTRODUCTION

The Breville smart air fryer oven is a very excellent kitchen appliance to own. It is very easy to use, has a superb blue smart screen to adjust the air fryer time and temperature. The Breville brand name is very trusted by all the families around the world and is a good brand to use. It is an excellent brand to own for a Breville smart air fryer review. Breville smart air fryer is also affordable and reliable. It lasts for a very long time and makes some delicious and tasty food.

On the other hand, you can get a new Breville air fryer for a Christmas present. So it remains an ideal Christmas present for your loved ones. So, it is an excellent kitchen appliance to own when you want to make tasty and delicious meals for your family. Just make sure that you buy the correct, authentic freezer when you get a Breville smart air fryer for your own. This is very important. There are so many fake, cheap air fryers that are already being sold but they are not great for quality. So, make sure you get the correct one for you.

Breville smart air fryer has been getting some excellent reviews for its performance. It has also been winning more and more awards for its excellent quality. It is very reliable and durable too. It last for a very long time so it is also very affordable and easy to use. It is not a heavy air fryer to carry around. It is a fantastic kitchen appliance to own and you can get it online now.

Don't miss out on this great deal. Get it now to make your next meal with it. It is really very user-friendly kitchen appliance to own.

Just make sure you buy the correct one when you want to get a Breville smart air fryer oven for your kitchen. So, make sure you buy the one with the serial number on it. You can easily check the serial number by highlighting the barcode of the item in the store. Then you can see the actual serial number in the discount price at the store. So, when you buy the correct, authentic air fryer in the store, you can see the authentic serial number. Make sure you understand this when you buy the Breville smart air fryer for your kitchen.

Moreover, you can look at this website for more information about it. This website is one of the best places to find detailed information about the Breville smart air fryer review and many more. Just make sure you buy the correct one for your kitchen. Make sure it is an authentic air fryer for your family.

Breville air fryer has been getting excellent rating from its users for its product quality. It is also receiving many excellent Breville air fryer reviews online. It has a long list of satisfied customers and all of them are recommending it with excellent rating. It is one of the best air fryers out there. If you want to get great quality air fryer for your family, then Breville air fryer is very lucrative. You can see for yourself after you use a Breville air fryer for a while. It is a very good air fryer and reliable. You can use it for a long time, and it will serve you very well for many years. So, if you want good quality air fryer then get a Breville air fryer now and have a tasty, delicious food for life.

So, don't hesitate and bring this great air fryer for your home for your cooking and eating. Go ahead and pack that air fryer for Christmas for your family. It is a great gift for them, and it can start making tasty, delicious meals for you. It can bring the taste of restaurants to your kitchen with great ease. So, if you are looking for a good air fryer for your kitchen and home, then get a Breville air fryer now from the store. Buy this new Breville air fryer at the store now and include a discount to choose the best for you. You can get this new air fryer for your family and loved ones very easily. It is an excellent Christmas gift and present you can get for them.

The Advantages of The Breville Smart Air Fryer Oven

The Breville smart air fryer oven is an all-in-one that allows cooking to be easy and quick. It also leads to a lot of possibilities once you get to know it. Once you learn the basics and become familiar with your Breville smart air fryer oven, you can feel free to experiment and modify the recipes in the way you prefer. You can prepare a wide number of dishes in the Breville smart air fryer oven and you can adapt your favorite stove-top dish so it becomes Breville smart air fryer oven–friendly. It all boils down to variety and lots of options, right? Here are some of the advantages of Breville Smart Air fryer:

The Breville smart air fryer has adjustable temperature settings

The Breville smart air fryer has adjustable temperature settings, so you will get to choose the heat level. The Breville smart air fryer has a range of temperature settings that you can choose from. The standard temperature options include 180 °C, 200 °C, 220 °C, 230 °C, and 240 °C. You can select any of these presets, depending on the dish that you want to prepare and how quickly you want to prepare it. If you cook quickly, then you might prefer to choose the higher settings and if you want to prolong the time of cooking or if you are in a hurry to complete the cooking process, then the lower temperature settings are better. None of the standard temperature settings will harm the food, so you can be quite relaxed as far as the temperature is concerned.

The Breville smart air fryer has adjustable timing settings

This is an advanced feature that a good number of Breville smart air fryer ovens come with. Breville smart air fryer ovens are quite advanced and offer a series of time settings. The Breville smart air fryer has preset time settings that you can choose from, in order to make the cooking process easier for you. Some of the Breville smart air fryer preset time settings include 30 seconds, 1 minute, 2 minutes, 5 minutes, 8 minutes, 10 minutes, and 15 minutes. All of these are easy to understand and easy to use for cooking. As a result, you can get to cook on a wide number of time settings and you will not have to think so much about the exact timing, at least not during the cooking process. As far as the time duration is concerned, it is better to experiment a little once you are familiar with the Breville smart air fryer, so you can get to select the timing that will suit your needs.

The Breville smart air fryer itself is dishwasher-safe

This is an important feature of the Breville smart air fryer. The Breville smart air fryer is dishwasher safe. Thus, you will never get challenged by the chore of stacking the dishes or getting cramps, while performing the dishwashing. The Breville smart air fryer has a removable cooking basket that can be taken out and placed in the dishwasher or it can be rinsed by hand if need be. Why is removable basket important? Well, usually, the removable basket of the Breville smart air fryer is dishwasher-safe, so you can load it in the dishwasher when you are done cooking because it is a part of the whole appliance and it is best to include the removable basket in the washing process

The Breville smart air fryer has an adjustable height

The Breville smart air fryer has an adjustable height. What does this mean? Well, with an adjustable height, means that you can easily adjust the height of the Breville smart air fryer to suit your preferences or your kitchen setup. The Breville smart air fryer has an adjustable height, so you can change the height, according to your needs and preferences. During the first few uses, you might want to perform a few trials and understand the most suitable height that suits you the most. The adjustable height is desirable, if you have a small waistline Breville smart air fryer because then you would get a Breville smart air fryer that you will find easier to stash away in your kitchen cabinet.

The Breville smart air fryer has a simple control system

The Breville smart air fryer has a simple control system. This means that the Breville smart air fryer has the easiest controls available on the market. Many Breville smart air fryer reviews regard this feature as one of the best features. With a simple control system, you will never have problems operating the Breville smart air fryer. You will not need to go through a series of long instructions. Instead, you can simply enter the heat level and/or the time setting that you want and the Breville smart air fryer will automatically get started.

The Breville smart air fryer is easy to operate

The Breville smart air fryer is easy to operate. Maintenance and cleaning are easy and straightforward. To clean the Breville smart air fryer, you can either use a dishwasher or hand wash it. There is no complicated process involved. In fact, there are many Breville smart air fryer owners who have not even tried to clean their Breville smart air fryer by hand because it was so easy to clean using the dishwasher. After using the Breville smart air fryer, you can simply detach the cooking basket and place it in the dishwasher. Other parts of the Breville smart air fryer can be hand cleaned.

The Breville smart air fryer is easy to assemble and use

The Breville smart air fryer is easy to assemble and it is easy to use. So, what does this mean? Well, you might have guessed it right. You will not have any complicated assembly processes when it comes to the Breville smart air fryer. The Breville smart air fryer comes in one single package that you will be able to open with ease when you get it. One of the best parts about this is that you won't have any complicated manuals or long instructions manuals to follow. If you have any doubts, visit the Breville smart air fryer reviews and you will get all the instructions and tips for using the Breville smart air fryer. Just as the Breville smart air fryer is easy to assemble, it is also easy to use. With a simple control system and a simple control system, you will never be lost.

The Breville smart air fryer is multifunctional

The Breville smart air fryer is multifunctional. This means that the Breville smart air fryer has a high level of versatility and you can do more than just cooking. First, of course, it has a convection cooking feature. This means that the Breville smart air fryer also lets you bake, roast and grill. The Breville smart air fryer also lets you keep food warm. So, for instance, if you want to keep the chicken warm before serving, you can accomplish that too with the Breville smart air fryer. You can also bake desserts such as pies with the Breville smart air fryer. That's going one step further than the multifunctional ability of the Brcville smart air fryer because you can heat up food and make desserts with the Breville smart air fryer. Cooking, grilling, roasting, and keeping food warm are the main functions of the Breville smart air fryer.

Benefits of The Air Fryer Oven

Energy and time efficient

One of the main advantages of breville smart air fryer oven is its ability to save time. Time is a vital resource for modern people, and everyone strives to do everything quickly and efficiently to save it. It cooks food by creating hot air inside the oven. This means that no overcooking, burning, or undercooking of food. The direct and even heat saves both time and energy and cooks food quickly. Another way to save time is to cook frozen foods without defrosting. You don't have to defrost food to room temperature before you cook it. Pick your frozen food out of the fridge, put it in the oven, set the right temperature, and you're good to go!

Capacious

Unlike other electric ovens, you will find breville smart air fryer oven much spacious and suitable to cook large

Serving sizes. The interior of the oven is large enough to carry large-sized baking pans.

User-friendly

There are no complex mechanisms to control the functional and operational keys of this oven. The control panel has the program's keys and the keys to adjust the time and temperature. The user can change the settings by a single press of the button and can also go for the default setting of each program.

Healthy cooking

Three types of temperatures can be used together to remove almost allFat from products. But at the same time, your meals remain tasty and juicy. Besides, thanks to fast cooking, food retains a large number of nutrients. This makes any dish cooked in breville smart air fryer oven useful and low-Fat.

It eliminates cooking odors through internal air filters.

Makes cleaning more manageable due to lack of oil or grease.

Air fryers can bake, grill, roast, and fry, providing more options.

A safer direction of cooking compared to deep frying with exposed hot oil.

How to Use the Breville Smart Air Fryer Oven?

Your air fryer oven really couldn't be easier to use. The following are some steps to help you get going!

Step 1: start by checking all the components of the breville smart air fryer oven and see if they are in good shape, especially the power cord, because any fault in the power cord can be hazardous.

Step 2: remove the air fryer oven from the box. Place it on a level surface near a grounded power outlet. Plug the air fryer oven.

Step 3: remove the trays from the oven. (before using the oven, make sure to clean the trays with soap and water thoroughly.) Right after unboxing the device, it is essential to clean the appliance inside out using a clean piece of cloth and wash all the removable accessories of the oven before the use.

Step4: set the oven to the pizza function and use the time button to select 18 minutes.

Step 5: press the start button and allow finishing the cooking cycle. Once the cooking cycle has finished, your breville smart oven is ready to use.

Learning the controls

The great thing about the breville smart air fryer oven is that all the controls are labeled for easy use, so you don't have to bother with confusing dials.

Function knob:

This knob allows you to select which cooking program you would like. Choose from toast, bake, broil, roast; cookies, reheat, pizza, and bagel.

Lcd display:

Displays the number of pieces of bread, darkness setting; current time; cooking temperature, and amount of time left to cook.

Temp/darkness button:

Select the temperature or darkness setting for the toast.

Up and down selection buttons:

Use to adjust time, temperature, and amount of darkness.

Time/slices button:

Use to adjust the cooking time and number of slices of bread.

A bit more:

This function adds a small amount of cooking time. The amount of time varies depending on which cooking program you have chosen.

Start/cancel button:

It starts and stops the cooking process.

F/c button:

Choose fahrenheit or celsius.

Frozen foods button:

Adds extra time to the cooking process to defrost frozen foods.

Pro tips

Defrosting

Defrosting food items can be a challenge and defrosting incorrectly can lead to unfortunate results. Ideally, the best way is to defrost food gradually and evenly, so that all of it defrosts at the same rate and to the same temperature. This is the best way to ensure even cooking. The breville smart air fryer oven features a specific frozen foods function that controls a low level of heat and circulates the air for even coverage before starting your cooking program. This way, your food will defrost quickly. Still, it will also be evenly defrosted and ready to cook using your preferred directions.

Avoid overcooking

While you may be familiar with cooking in a conventional oven, an air fryer oven works a little bit differently. First of all, it's much smaller, which means two things: it heats up a lot faster, and it retains heat very well. As a result, many users find that if they follow the temperature and time settings for dishes meant to be cooked in conventional ovens, their food overcooks.

Aluminum foil

Using aluminum foil in the breville smart air fryer oven is not a good idea. The problem is that using aluminum foil can cause the oven to get too hot - sometimes over 500°f and an air fryer oven, unlike your conventional oven, isn't designed to work at such a high temperature safely. To combat this problem and still have a way to line the trays of your air fryer oven, try using parchment paper. It will keep food from sticking to the trays, and you can just throw it out after cooking.

Safety

When removing items from the oven, always be sure to wear oven mitts and use the side handles to move the oven when hot.

When opening the door of the oven, make sure your face keeps a safe distance from it, as the oven will be very hot after cooking.

Cleaning

After the oven has had a chance to cool; clean it using a damp cloth or sponge to remove any spatter that may have occurred during the cooking process.

CHAPTER 2:

BREAKFAST AND BRUNCH RECIPES

1. Healthy Sushi Rolls Salad

Preparation time: 1 hour 15 minutes

Preparation time: 10 minutes

Cooking time: 10 minutes

Servings: 3

INGREDIENTS

For the salad:

- 1 ½ cups young kale with the stem removed
- 1 tbsp. Toasted sesame seeds
- ¼ tsp. Ginger powder
- 1 pinch garlic powder
- ½ tsp. Sesame oil
- 1/2 -3/4 tsp. Soy sauce
- ½ tsp. Rice vinegar

For the sushi rolls:

- 1 cup sushi rice, at room temperature
- ½ an avocado, thinly sliced
- 3 sheets of nori

- ¼ cup mayonnaise
- Sriracha sauce
- ¾ cup panko breadcrumbs

DIRECTIONS

1. Combine all the salad ingredients in a large bowl except for the sesame seeds. With wet hands, rub the kale until it wilts and turns bright green then toss in the sesame seeds until well combined and set aside.

2. For the rolls, spread out the nori sheets, one at a time on a clean and dry surface. Wet your hands and shake off the excess water. Place a handful of rice on the spread out sheet to make a thin layer of rice but leave out about an inch on one side of the sheet, to make the seal.

3. Place two tablespoons on one edge of the sheet ant top with a few avocado slices. Gently but tightly roll up the sushi and seal with the uncovered end. Wet your fingertips to help the flap hold better.

4. Repeat this process for the remaining nori sheets.

5. In a small bowl, combine the mayonnaise with the sriracha sauce a little at a time until you reach your desired spice level.

6. Next put your breadcrumbs in a large, shallow bowl. Coat one of the sushi rolls with the mayo mixture and gently coat with the breadcrumbs until evenly coated. Do the same for the remaining two rolls.

7. Set your air fryer toast oven at 390 degrees f and cook the rolls for 10 minutes, turning the rolls gently halfway through cooking time: .

8. Remove the rolls and set on a cutting board and cut each roll (in a gentle motion to avoid spilling the contents) into about 6 rolls.

9. Use soy sauce or other favorite sauce as your dip. Enjoy!

NUTRITION: Calories: 632 K Cal, Carbs: 32.2 g, Fat: 11.2 g, Protein: 18.9 g.

2. **Feta & Mushroom Frittata**

Preparation Time: 30 minutes

Servings: 4

INGREDIENTS

- 1 red onion, thinly sliced

- 4 cups button mushrooms, thinly sliced

- Salt to taste

- 6 tablespoons feta cheese, crumbled

- 6 medium eggs

- Non-stick cooking spray

- 2 tablespoons olive oil

DIRECTIONS

1. Sauté the onion and mushrooms in olive oil over medium heat until the vegetables are tender. Remove the vegetables from pan and drain on a paper towel-lined plate. In a mixing bowl, whisk eggs and salt. Coat all sides of baking dish with cooking spray. Preheat your air fryer to 325°Fahrenheit. Pour the beaten eggs into prepared baking dish and scatter the sautéed vegetables and crumble feta on top. Bake in the air fryer for 30-minutes. Allow to cool slightly and serve!

Nutritional Values per serving: Calories: 226, Total Fat: 9.3g, Carbs: 8.7g, Protein: 12.6g

3. Hot Fried Breakfast Cabbage Patties

Preparation Time: 15 minutes

Servings: 4

INGREDIENTS

- 4 eggs, beaten

- 2 cups, shredded purple cabbage

- 1 cup cornmeal

- Pinch of sea salt

- 1 tablespoon onion powder

- 1 tablespoon olive oil

- 1 teaspoon black pepper

DIRECTIONS

1. Preheat your air fryer to 390°Fahrenheit. Blend all the ingredients except olive oil, in a bowl. Grease heat-safe dish with olive oil. Spoon the mixture into dish and form patties. Add patties to heat-safe dish and cook in air fryer for 15-minutes. Serve as a vegetarian breakfast burger.

Nutritional Values per serving: Calories: 221, Total Fat: 9.4g, Carbs: 8.6g, Protein: 14.2g

CHAPTER 3:

MAINS AIR-FRIED

4. Minced Beef Kebab Skewers

Preparation Time: 25 minutes

Servings: 2

INGREDIENTS

- ½ lb. of minced beef
- ½ large onion, chopped
- 1 medium green chili
- ½ teaspoon chili powder
- 1 clove of garlic, minced
- 1 pinch of ginger
- 1 teaspoon Garam Masala
- 3 tablespoons of pork rinds

DIRECTIONS

1. Grate the ginger and garlic. Chop and deseed the chili. Chop the onion. Mix the ginger, chili, and onion with the minced beef. Add the powdered spices. Add a few pork rinds and salt. Shape the beef into Fat sausages around short wooden skewers. Set the skewers aside for an hour, then cook them in your preheated air fryer for 25-minutes at 350°Fahrenheit.

5. **Pomfret Fish Fry**

Preparation Time: 15-minutes

Servings: 5

INGREDIENTS

- 4 onions

- 3 lbs. of silver Pomfret

- Salt and black pepper to taste

- 2 tablespoons olive oil

- 2 teaspoons lemon juice

- 3 pinches of cumin powder

- ¾ teaspoons of ginger

- 3 pinches of red chili powder

- 1 tablespoon turmeric powder

- 1 teaspoon garlic paste

DIRECTIONS

1. Wash the fish with clean water and soak it in lemon juice to remove any unpleasant smell. After 30-minutes, take the fish out and wash it with clean water. Draw diagonal shaped slits on the fish. Combine the black pepper, salt, lemon juice, garlic paste, and turmeric powder. Rub the mixture inside and outside of fish and leave it in the fridge for 30-minutes to absorb the seasoning. Add the fish to air fryer basket with 2 tablespoons olive oil and cook for 12-minutes at 340°Fahrenheit.

Nutritional Values per serving: Calories: 278, Total Fat: 8.6g, Carbs: 7.4g, Protein: 32g

6. <u>Cedar Planked Salmon</u>

Preparation Time: 15 minutes

Servings: 6

INGREDIENTS

- 4 untreated cedar planks
- ½ cup olive oil
- 1 ½ tablespoons of rice vinegar
- 1 teaspoon sesame oil
- 2 lbs. of salmon fillets, skin removed
- 1 teaspoon garlic, minced
- 1 tablespoon ginger root, fresh, grated
- ¼ cup green onions, chopped
- ½ cup soy sauce

DIRECTIONS

1. Start by soaking the cedar planks for 2-hours. Take a shallow baking dish and stir in the olive oil, the rice vinegar, the sesame oil, soy sauce, ginger, and green onions. Place the salmon fillets in the prepared marinade for at least 20-minutes. Place the planks in the basket of your air fryer. Cook the salmon fillets for 15-minutes at 360°Fahrenheit.

Nutritional Values per serving: Calories: 273, Total Fat: 7.5g, Carbs: 5.2g, Protein: 34.2g

7. **Crested Halibut**

Preparation Time: 30 minutes

Servings: 4

INGREDIENTS

- 4 halibut fillets

- ¾ cup of pork rinds

- ½ cup of parsley, fresh, chopped

- ¼ cup dill, fresh, chopped

- ¼ cup chives, fresh, chopped

- 1 tablespoon olive oil

- 1 teaspoon lemon zest, finely grated

- Sea salt and black pepper to taste

DIRECTIONS

1. Preheat your air fryer to 390°Fahrenheit. In a mixing bowl, combine the pork rinds, parsley, dill, chives, olive oil, lemon zest, sea salt and black pepper. Rinse the halibut fillets and dry them on a paper towel. Arrange the halibut fillets and dry them on a paper towel. Arrange the halibut fillets onto a baking sheet. Spoon the pork rind crumb mixture onto fish fillets. Lightly press the mixture on the fillets. Bake the fillets in your preheated air fryer basket for 30-minutes. Serve warm.

Nutritional Values per serving: Calories: 272, Total Fat: 10.3g, Carbs: 9.4g, Protein: 32.2g

8. Creamy Halibut

Preparation Time: 20 minutes

Servings: 6

INGREDIENTS

- 2 lbs. of halibut fillets, cut into 6 pieces
- 1 teaspoon dill weed, dried
- ½ cup light sour cream
- ½ cup light mayonnaise
- 4-chopped green onions

DIRECTIONS

1. Preheat the air fryer to 390°Fahrenheit. Season the halibut with salt and pepper. In a bowl, mix the onions, sour cream, mayonnaise, and dill. Spread the onion mixture evenly over the halibut fillets. Cook in air fryer for 20-minutes. Serve warm.

Nutritional Values per serving: Calories: 286, Total Fat: 11.3g, Carbs: 6.9, Protein: 29.8g

9. **Air Fried Catfish**

Preparation Time: 20 minutes

Servings: 2

INGREDIENTS

- 5 catfish filets
- 1 pinch of salt
- 1 teaspoon garlic powder
- 1 teaspoon crab seasoning
- 1 cup almond flour
- 2 tablespoons olive oil for spraying
- 2 tablespoons hot sauce
- 1 cup buttermilk
- Black pepper as needed

DIRECTIONS

1. Season catfish fillets on both sides with salt and pepper. In a dish, combine the buttermilk with hot sauce. Add the catfish fillets and cover them with liquid. Let the ingredients soak while you prepare the rest of the ingredients. Whisk the flour, crab seasoning, and garlic powder in a casserole dish. Remove the catfish from the buttermilk and allow excess liquid to drip off. Dredge the catfish on both sides in the flour mixture. Place fillets into air fryer and drizzle with oil. Cook at 390°Fahrenheit for 15-minutes. When cooking is completed remove basket and

gently turn the fillets over, spray some oil on them, and cook for an additional 5-minutes.

Nutritional Values per serving: Calories: 283, Total Fat: 8.6g, Carbs: 6.5g, Protein: 34.3g

10. Roasted Chicken Legs

Preparation Time: 35 minutes

Servings: 2

INGREDIENTS

- 2 chicken legs
- 2 teaspoons sweet smoked paprika
- 1 teaspoon honey
- Salt and pepper to taste
- ½ teaspoon garlic powder
- Fresh parsley, chopped for garnish
- 1 lime sliced for garnish

DIRECTIONS

1. Combine all the ingredients except the chicken in a bowl.
2. Rub the mixture over the chicken and preheat your air fryer for 3-minutes.
3. Cook the chicken in air fryer at 390°Fahrenheit for 35-minutes.
4. Serve with a favorite salad of your choice.

Nutritional Values per serving: Calories: 232, Total Fat: 9.3g, Carbs: 7.5g, Protein: 22.1g

CHAPTER 4:

POULTRY

11. Cheesy Chicken Lasagna

Preparation time: 10 minutes

Cooking time: 45 minutes

Servings: 9

INGREDIENTS

- 3 cups chicken, cooked and diced
- 1/2 cup onion, chopped
- 8 lasagna noodles, cooked and drained
- 1/2 cup green bell pepper, chopped
- 1/2 cup parmesan cheese, grated
- 1/2 tsp dried basil
- 2 cups processed cheese, shredded
- 16 oz cottage cheese
- 6 oz can mushroom, drained and sliced
- 10 oz can cream of chicken soup
- 1/4 cup pimento peppers, chopped
- 3/4 cup milk
- 3 tbsp butter

DIRECTIONS

1. Insert wire rack in rack position 6. Select bake, set temperature 350 f, timer for 45 minutes. Press start to preheat the oven.

2. Melt butter in a saucepan over medium heat. Add bell pepper, onion and sauté.

3. Stir in soup, pimento, basil, processed cheese, milk, and mushrooms.

4. Place 1/2 noodles in a baking dish then layer with 1/2 cream sauce, half cottage cheese, half chicken, and half parmesan cheese. Repeat layers.

5. Bake for 45 minutes.

6. Serve and enjoy.

NUTRITION: Calories449, Fat 16.8 g, Carbohydrates 38.8 g, Sugar 3.8 g, Protein35 g, Cholesterol 96 mg

12. Parmesan Chicken & Veggies

Preparation time: 10 minutes

Cooking time: 30 minutes

Servings: 4

INGREDIENTS

- 4 chicken breasts, skinless and boneless
- 2 tbsp olive oil
- 1/2 tsp garlic powder
- 1/2 cup parmesan cheese, grated
- 1/2 cup Italian seasoned breadcrumbs
- 4 tbsp butter, melted
- 1/2 lb. baby potatoes cut into fourths
- 1 yellow squash, sliced
- 1 zucchini, sliced
- Pepper
- Salt

DIRECTIONS

1. Spray a baking dish with cooking spray and set aside.
2. Insert wire rack in rack position 6. Select bake, set temperature 350 f, timer for 30 minutes. Press start to preheat the oven.
3. Place melted butter in a shallow dish.
4. In another dish mix together, parmesan cheese, breadcrumbs, and garlic powder.

5. Season chicken with pepper and salt then dip into the melted butter and coat with cheese mixture.

6. Place coated chicken in a baking dish.

7. In mixing bowl, add potatoes, yellow squash, zucchini, and olive oil toss well.

8. Add vegetables into the baking dish around the chicken and bake for 30 minutes.

9. Serve and enjoy.

NUTRITION: Calories 579, Fat 32.7 g, Carbohydrates 20.4 g, Sugar 2.3 g, Protein50.2 g, Cholesterol 169 mg

13. <u>Chicken Cheese Rice</u>

Preparation time: 10 minutes

Cooking time: 25 minutes

Servings: 4

INGREDIENTS

- 1 cup chicken breast, cooked and shredded
- 2 tbsp all-purpose flour
- 2 cup cooked brown rice
- 1 tbsp garlic, minced
- 2 tbsp butter
- 1 cup cheddar cheese, shredded
- 1 cup chicken stock
- 1/2 tbsp fresh thyme, chopped
- 1/2 tsp pepper
- 1/1 tsp salt

DIRECTIONS

1. Spray a baking dish with cooking spray and set aside.
2. Insert wire rack in rack position 6. Select bake, set temperature 350 f, timer for 25 minutes. Press start to preheat the oven.
3. Melt butter in a pan over medium-high heat. Add garlic and cook for 1 minute. Add thyme, pepper, salt, and flour stir well.
4. Pour chicken stock into the pan and whisk constantly. Whisk until thick then add cheese and stir until melted.

5. Add chicken and cooked rice stir well to combine. Transfer pan mixture into the baking dish and bake for 25 minutes.

6. Serve and enjoy.

NUTRITION: Calories559, Fat 18.5 g, Carbohydrates 77 g, Sugar 0.4 g, Protein20.3 g, Cholesterol 61 mg

14. Chicken Kabab

Preparation time: 10 minutes

Cooking time: 6 minutes

Servings: 3

INGREDIENTS

- 1 lb. ground chicken
- 1/4 cup almond flour
- 2 green onion, chopped
- 1 egg, lightly beaten
- 1/3 cup fresh parsley, chopped
- 2 garlic cloves
- 4 oz onion, chopped
- 1/4 tsp turmeric powder
- 1/2 tsp black pepper
- 1 tbsp fresh lemon juice

DIRECTIONS

1. Insert wire rack in rack position 4. Select air fry, set temperature 400 f, timer for 6 minutes. Press start to preheat the oven.
2. Add all ingredients into the food processor and process until well combined.
3. Transfer chicken mixture to the bowl and place it in the refrigerator for 30 minutes.
4. Divide mixture into the 6 equal portions and roll around the soaked wooden skewers.

5. Place kabab into the air fryer basket air fry for 6 minutes.

6. Serve and enjoy.

NUTRITION: Calories 391, Fat 17.3 g, Carbohydrates 7.9 g, Sugar 2.1 g, Protein 48.6 g, Cholesterol 189 mg

CHAPTER 5:

SEAFOOD RECIPES

15. Steamed Salmon & Sauce

Preparation time: 10 minutes

Cooking time: 10 minutes

Servings: 2

INGREDIENTS

- 1 cup water
- 2 x 6 oz fresh salmon
- 2 tsp vegetable oil
- A pinch of salt for each fish
- ½ cup plain Greek yogurt
- ½ cup sour cream
- 2 tbsp finely chopped dill (keep a bit for garnishing)
- A pinch of salt to taste

DIRECTIONS

1. Pour the water into the tray of the Beeville air fryer oven and start heating to 285° f.
2. Drizzle oil over the fish and spread it. Salt the fish to taste.
3. Now pop it into the Beeville air fryer oven for 10 min.

4. In the meantime, mix the yogurt, cream, dill and a bit of salt to make the sauce. When the fish is done, serve with the sauce and garnish with sprigs of dill.

NUTRITION: Calories 296, Fat 11.5 g, Carbohydrates 18.7 g, Sugar 0.9 g, Protein29.9 g, Cholesterol 171 mg

16. <u>Sweet And Savory Breaded Shrimp</u>

Preparation time: 10 minutes

Cooking time: 20 minutes

Servings: 2

INGREDIENTS

- ½ pound of fresh shrimp, peeled from their shells and rinsed
- 2 raw eggs
- ½ cup of breadcrumbs (we like panko, but any brand or home recipe will do)
- ½ white onion, peeled and rinsed and finely chopped
- 1 teaspoon of ginger-garlic paste
- ½ teaspoon of turmeric powder
- ½ teaspoon of red chili powder
- ½ teaspoon of cumin powder
- ½ teaspoon of black pepper powder
- ½ teaspoon of dry mango powder
- Pinch of salt

DIRECTIONS

1. Cover the basket of the air fryer with a lining of tin foil, leaving the edges uncovered to allow air to circulate through the basket.
2. Preheat the Beeville air fryer oven to 350 degrees.
3. In a large mixing bowl, beat the eggs until fluffy and until the yolks and whites are fully combined.
4. Dunk all the shrimp in the egg mixture, fully submerging.

5. In a separate mixing bowl, combine the breadcrumbs with all the dry ingredients until evenly blended.

6. One by one, coat the egg-covered shrimp in the mixed dry ingredients so that fully covered, and place on the foil-lined air-fryer basket.

7. Set the Beeville air fryer oven timer to 20 minutes.

8. Halfway through the cooking time, shake the handle of the air-fryer so that the breaded shrimp jostles inside and fry-coverage is even.

9. After 20 minutes, when the fryer shuts off, the shrimp will be perfectly cooked and their breaded crust golden-brown and delicious! Using tongs, remove from the air fryer and set on a

10. Serving dish to cool.

NUTRITION: Calories 296, Fat 11.5 g, Carbohydrates 18.7 g, Sugar 0.9 g ,Protein29.9 g ,Cholesterol 171 mg

CHAPTER 6:

BEEF, LAMB AND PORK RECIPES

17. Cheeseburger Egg Rolls

Preparation time: 10 minutes

Cooking time: 7 minutes

Servings: 6

INGREDIENTS

- 6 egg roll wrappers
- 6 chopped dill pickle chips
- 1 tbsp. Yellow mustard
- 3 tbsp. Cream cheese
- 3 tbsp. Shredded cheddar cheese
- ½ c. Chopped onion
- ½ c. Chopped bell pepper
- ¼ tsp. Onion powder
- ¼ tsp. Garlic powder
- 8 ounces of raw lean ground beef

DIRECTIONS

1. In a skillet, add seasonings, beef, onion, and bell pepper. Stir and crumble beef till fully cooked, and vegetables are soft.

2. Take skillet off the heat and add cream cheese, mustard, and cheddar cheese, stirring till melted.

3. Pour beef mixture into a bowl and fold in pickles.

4. Lay out egg wrappers and place 1/6th of beef mixture into each one. Moisten egg roll wrapper edges with water. Fold sides to the middle and seal with water.

5. Repeat with all other egg rolls.

6. Place rolls into air fryer, one batch at a time.

7. Pour into the oven rack/basket. Place the rack on the middle-shelf of the Breville air fryer oven. Set temperature to 392°f and set time to 7 minutes.

NUTRITION: Calories: 153; Fat: 4g; Protein:12g; sugar:3g

18. Air Fried Grilled Steak

Preparation time: 10 minutes

Cooking time: 45 minutes

Servings: 2

INGREDIENTS

- 2 top sirloin steaks

- 3 tablespoons butter, melted

- 3 tablespoons olive oil

- Salt and pepper to taste

DIRECTIONS

1. Preheat the Breville air fryer oven for 5 minutes.

2. Season the sirloin steaks with olive oil, salt and pepper.

3. Place the beef in the air fryer basket.

4. Cook for 45 minutes at 350°f.

5. Once cooked, serve with butter.

NUTRITION: Calories: 1536; Fat: 123.7g; Protein:103.4g

19. Juicy Cheeseburgers

Preparation time: 10 minutes

Cooking time: 15 minutes

Servings: 4

INGREDIENTS

- 1 pound 93% lean ground beef

- 1 teaspoon Worcestershire sauce

- 1 tablespoon burger seasoning

- Salt

- Pepper

- Cooking oil

- 4 slices cheese

- Buns

DIRECTIONS

1. In a large bowl, mix the ground beef, Worcestershire, burger seasoning, and salt and pepper to taste until well blended. Spray the air fryer basket with cooking oil. You will need only a quick spritz. The burgers will produce oil as they cook. Shape the mixture into 4 patties. Place the burgers in the air fryer. The burgers should fit without the need to stack, but stacking is okay if necessary.

2. Pour into the oven rack/basket. Place the rack on the middle-shelf of the Breville air fryer oven. Set temperature to 375°f and set time to 8 minutes. Cook for 8 minutes. Open the air fryer and flip the burgers. Cook for an additional 3 to 4 minutes.

Check the inside of the burgers to determine if they have finished cooking. You can stick a knife or fork in the center to examine the color.

3. Top each burger with a slice of cheese. Cook for an additional minute, or until the cheese has melted. Serve on buns with any additional toppings of your choice.

NUTRITION: Calories: 566; Fat: 39g; Protein:29g; Fiber :1g

20. Spicy Thai Beef Stir-Fry

Preparation time: 10 minutes

Cooking time: 9 minutes

Servings: 4

INGREDIENTS

- 1-pound sirloin steaks, thinly sliced
- 2 tablespoons lime juice, divided
- ⅓ cup crunchy peanut butter
- ½ cup beef broth
- 1 tablespoon olive oil
- 1½ cups broccoli florets
- 2 cloves garlic, sliced
- 1 to 2 red chile peppers, sliced

DIRECTIONS

1. In a medium bowl, combine the steak with 1 tablespoon of the lime juice. Set aside.

2. Combine the peanut butter and beef broth in a small bowl and mix well. Drain the beef and add the juice from the bowl into the peanut butter mixture.

3. In a 6-inch metal bowl, combine the olive oil, steak, and broccoli.

4. Pour into the oven rack/basket. Place the rack on the middle-shelf of the Breville air fryer oven. Set temperature to 375°f and set time to 4 minutes. Cook for 3 to 4 minutes or until the steak

is almost cooked and the broccoli is crisp and tender, shaking the basket once during cooking time.

5. Add the garlic, chile peppers, and the peanut butter mixture and stir.

6. Cook for 3 to 5 minutes or until the sauce is bubbling and the broccoli is tender.

7. Serve over hot rice.

NUTRITION: Calories: 387; Fat: 22g; Protein:42g; Fiber :2g

21. <u>Beef Brisket Recipe From Texas</u>

Preparation time: 10 minutes

Cooking time: 1hour and 30 minutes

Servings: 8

INGREDIENTS

- 1 ½ cup beef stock
- 1 bay leaf
- 1 tablespoon garlic powder
- 1 tablespoon onion powder
- 2 pounds beef brisket, trimmed
- 2 tablespoons chili powder
- 2 teaspoons dry mustard
- 4 tablespoons olive oil
- Salt and pepper to taste

DIRECTIONS

1. Preheat the Breville air fryer oven for 5 minutes. Place all ingredients in a deep baking dish that will fit in the air fryer.
2. Bake for 1 hour and 30 minutes at 400°f.
3. Stir the beef every after 30 minutes to soak in the sauce.

NUTRITION: Calories: 306; Fat: 24.1g; Protein:18.3g

22. <u>Copycat Taco Bell Crunch Wraps</u>

Preparation time: 10 minutes

Cooking time: 2 minutes

Servings: 6

INGREDIENTS

- 6 wheat tostadas
- 2 c. Sour cream
- 2 c. Mexican blend cheese
- 2 c. Shredded lettuce
- 12 ounces low-sodium nacho cheese
- 3 roma tomatoes
- 6 12-inch wheat tortillas
- 1 1/3 c. Water
- 2 packets low-sodium taco seasoning
- 2 pounds of lean ground beef

DIRECTIONS

1. Ensure your air fryer is preheated to 400 degrees.
2. Make beef according to taco seasoning packets.
3. Place 2/3 c. Prepared beef, 4 tbsp. Cheese, 1 tostada, 1/3 c. Sour cream, 1/3 c. Lettuce, 1/6th of tomatoes and 1/3 c. Cheese on each tortilla.
4. Fold up tortillas edges and repeat with remaining ingredients.
5. Lay the folded sides of tortillas down into the air fryer and spray with olive oil.

6. Set temperature to 400°f and set time to 2 minutes. Cook 2 minutes till browned.

NUTRITION: Calories: 311; Fat: 9g; Protein:22g; sugar:2g

23. Air Fryer Burgers

Preparation time: 10 minutes

Cooking time: 10 minutes

Servings: 4

INGREDIENTS

- 1-pound lean ground beef
- 1 tsp. Dried parsley
- ½ tsp. Dried oregano
- ½ tsp. Pepper
- ½ tsp. Salt
- ½ tsp. Onion powder
- ½ tsp. Garlic powder
- Few drops of liquid smoke
- 1 tsp. Worcestershire sauce

DIRECTIONS

1. Ensure your Breville air fryer oven is preheated to 350 degrees.
2. Mix all seasonings together till combined.
3. Place beef in a bowl and add seasonings. Mix well, but do not overmix.
4. Make 4 patties from the mixture and using your thumb, making an indent in the center of each patty.
5. Add patties to air fryer basket.
6. Set temperature to 350°f, and set time to 10 minutes, and cook 10 minutes. No need to turn.

NUTRITION: Calories: 148; Fat: 5g; Protein:24g; sugar:1g

CHAPTER 7:

SIDE DISH RECIPES

24. Hot Green Beans

Preparation time: 5 minutes

Cooking time: 20 minutes

Servings: 4

INGREDIENTS

- 6 cups green beans, trimmed
- 2 tablespoons olive oil
- 1 tablespoon hot paprika
- A pinch of salt and black pepper

DIRECTIONS

1. In a bowl, mix the green beans with the other ingredients, toss, put them in the air fryer's basket and cook at 370 degrees F for 20 minutes.
2. Divide between plates and serve as a side dish.

NUTRITION: Calories120, Fat 5, Fiber 1, Carbs 4, Protein2

25. Balsamic Asparagus

Preparation time: 5 minutes

Cooking time: 20 minutes

Servings: 4

INGREDIENTS

- 1-pound asparagus stalks

- Salt and black pepper to the taste

- ¼ cup olive oil+ 1 teaspoon

- 1 tablespoon smoked paprika

- 2 tablespoons balsamic vinegar

- 1 tablespoon lime juice

DIRECTIONS

1. In a bowl, mix the asparagus with salt, pepper and 1 teaspoon oil, toss, transfer to your air fryer's basket and cook at 370 degrees F for 20 minutes.

2. Meanwhile, in a bowl, mix all the other ingredients and whisk them well.

3. Divide the asparagus between plates, drizzle the balsamic vinaigrette all over and serve as a side dish.

NUTRITION: Calories187, Fat 6, Fiber 2, Carbs 4, Protein9

26. Garlic Asparagus

Preparation time: 5 minutes

Cooking time: 15 minutes

Servings: 4

INGREDIENTS

- 1 bunch asparagus, trimmed
- Salt and black pepper to the taste
- 4 tablespoons olive oil
- 4 garlic cloves, minced
- Juice of ½ lemon
- 3 tablespoons parmesan, grated

DIRECTIONS

1. In a bowl, mix the asparagus with all the ingredients except the parmesan, toss, transfer it to your air fryer's basket and cook at 400 degrees F for 15 minutes.
2. Divide between plates, sprinkle the parmesan on top and serve as a side dish.

NUTRITION: Calories173, Fat 12, Fiber 2, Carbs 5, Protein7

27. Collard Greens Sauté

Preparation time: 5 minutes

Cooking time: 15 minutes

Servings: 4

INGREDIENTS

- 1-pound collard greens
- ¼ cup cherry tomatoes, halved
- 1 tablespoon balsamic vinegar
- A pinch of salt and black pepper
- 2 tablespoons chicken stock

DIRECTIONS

1. In a pan that fits your air fryer, mix the collard greens with the other ingredients, toss gently, introduce in the air fryer and cook at 360 degrees F for 15 minutes.
2. Divide between plates and serve as a side dish.

NUTRITION: Calories121, Fat 3, Fiber 4, Carbs 6, Protein5

CHAPTER 8:

BEANS AND GRAINS RECIPES

28. Creamy Beans Mix

Preparation time: 5 minutes

Cooking time: 25 minutes

Servings: 4

INGREDIENTS

- 2 cups canned white beans, drained
- 1 cup heavy cream
- ½ teaspoon turmeric powder
- 1 teaspoon fennel seeds
- ½ teaspoon garam masala
- A pinch of salt and black pepper

DIRECTIONS

1. In the air fryer's pan, mix the beans with the cream and the other ingredients, put the pan in the machine and cook at 380 degrees F for 25 minutes.
2. Divide between plates and serve.

NUTRITION: Calories200, Fat 12, Fiber 2.3, Carbs 5.5, Protein4.3

29. Walnuts Bulgur Mix

Preparation time: 5 minutes

Cooking time: 25 minutes

Servings: 4

INGREDIENTS

- 1 cup bulgur
- 2 teaspoons olive oil
- ½ cup walnuts, chopped
- 2 garlic cloves, minced
- 1 cup veggie stock
- 1 tablespoon soy sauce
- Salt and black pepper to the taste
- 1 tablespoon chives, chopped

DIRECTIONS

1. In the air fryer's pan, mix the bulgur with the oil and the other ingredients, toss, put the pan in the fryer and cook at 370 degrees F for 25 minutes.
2. Divide everything between plates and serve.

NUTRITION: Calories233, Fat 3, Fiber 3.4, Carbs 12, Protein4

30. Minty Bulgur

Preparation time: 5 minutes

Cooking time: 25 minutes

Servings: 4

INGREDIENTS

- 1 red onion, chopped

- 1 cup bulgur

- 1 cup veggie stock

- 1 tablespoon mint, chopped

- Salt and black pepper to the taste

- ½ teaspoon ginger, grated

- 2 garlic cloves, minced

- 1 tablespoon lemon juice

- ½ cup walnuts, toasted and chopped

DIRECTIONS

1. In your air fryer's pan, mix the bulgur with the onion, stock and the other ingredients, toss, put the pan in the machine and cook at 370 degrees F for 25 minutes.

2. Divide between plates and serve.

NUTRITION: Calories263, Fat 12, Fiber 4, Carbs 8.9, Protein4

31. Green Lentils Mix

Preparation time: 10 minutes

Cooking time: 25 minutes

Servings: 4

INGREDIENTS

- 2 cups canned green lentils
- 2 cups chicken stock
- 3 spring onions, chopped
- 1 cup red bell pepper, chopped
- ½ cup zucchinis, cubed
- 1 tablespoon chives, chopped
- Salt and black pepper to the taste
- ½ teaspoon Italian seasoning

DIRECTIONS

1. In your air fryer, mix the lentils with the stock, spring onions and the other ingredients, toss, and cook at 370 degrees F for 25 minutes.
2. Divide the mix between plate sand serve.

NUTRITION: Calories232, Fat 12, Fiber 3, Carbs 8, Protein3.4

CHAPTER 9:

VEGETABLE RECIPES

32. Baked Sweet Potatoes

Preparation time: 10 minutes

Cooking time: 40 minutes

Servings: 4

INGREDIENTS

- 4 sweet potatoes, scrubbed and washed
- ½ tbsp. Butter, melted
- ½ tsp sea salt

DIRECTIONS

1. Prick sweet potatoes using a fork.
2. Rub sweet potatoes with melted butter and season with salt.
3. Arrange sweet potatoes on instant vortex air fryer drip pan and bake at 400 f for 40 minutes.
4. Serve and enjoy.

NUTRITION: Calories: 125 Cal Total Fat: 1.5 g   Saturated Fat: 0 g   Cholesterol: 4 mg   Sodium: 0 mg   Total Carbs: 26.2 g   Fiber: 0 g Sugar: 5.4 g   Protein: 2.1 g

33. Herbed Roasted Carrots

Preparation time: 10 minutes

Cooking time: 10 minutes

Servings: 4

INGREDIENTS

- 1-pound heirloom carrots, peeled
- 2 tablespoons fresh thyme, chopped finely
- 1 tablespoon fresh tarragon leaves, chopped finely
- 2 teaspoons olive oil
- Salt and ground black pepper, as required

DIRECTIONS

1. Place the carrots, herbs, oil, salt and black pepper in a bowl and toss to coat well
2. Arrange the greased "inner basket" in air fryer toaster oven and press "preheat".
3. Select "start/cancel" to begin preheating.
4. When the unit beeps to show that it is preheated, arrange the carrots in "inner basket".
5. Insert the "inner basket" and select "root vegetables".
6. Set the temperature to 400 degrees f for 10 minutes.
7. Select "start/cancel" to begin cooking.
8. Shake the carrots once halfway through.
9. Select "start/cancel" to stop cooking.

10. Serve hot.

NUTRITION: Calories: 72 Cal Total Fat: 2.5 g   Saturated Fat: 0.4 g   Cholesterol: 0 mg   Sodium: 118 mg   Total Carbs: 12.2 g   Fiber: 3.3 g   Sugar: 0 g   Protein: 1.2 g Potassium: 387 mg

34. Glazed Carrots

Preparation time: 10 minutes

Cooking time: 12 minutes

Servings: 4

INGREDIENTS

- 3 cups carrots, peeled and cut into large chunks
- 1 tablespoon olive oil
- 1 tablespoon honey
- 1 tablespoon fresh thyme, finely chopped
- Salt and ground black pepper, as required

DIRECTIONS

1. In a bowl, place all ingredients and toss to coat well.
2. Place the carrot mixture into a greased baking pan.
3. Arrange the "inner basket" in air fryer toaster oven and press "preheat".
4. Select "start/cancel" to begin preheating.
5. When the unit beeps to show that it is preheated, arrange the baking pan in "inner basket".
6. Insert the "inner basket" and select "air fry".
7. Set the temperature to 390 degrees f for 12 minutes.
8. Select "start/cancel" to begin cooking.
9. Select "start/cancel" to stop cooking.

10. Serve hot.

NUTRITION: Calories: 82 Cal Total Fat: 3.6 g   Saturated Fat: 0 g   Cholesterol: 0 mg   Sodium: 96 mg   Total Carbs: 12.9 g   Fiber: 2.3 g   Sugar: 8.4 g   Protein: 0.8 g   Potassium: 272 mg

35. Buttery Roasted Potatoes

Preparation time: 10 minutes

Cooking time: 20 minutes

Servings: 4

INGREDIENTS

- 1½ pounds of small new potatoes, halved

- 3 tablespoons butter, melted

- ¼ teaspoon dried thyme

- ¼ teaspoon dried rosemary

- ½ teaspoon garlic powder

- Salt and ground black pepper, as required

DIRECTIONS

1. In a large bowl, add all the ingredients and toss to coat well.

2. Arrange the greased "inner basket" in air fryer toaster oven and press "preheat".

3. Select "start/cancel" to begin preheating.

4. When the unit beeps to show that it is preheated, arrange the potatoes in "inner basket".

5. Insert the "inner basket" and select "french fries".

6. Set the temperature to 380 degrees f for 20 minutes.

7. Select "start/cancel" to begin cooking.

8. Shake the potatoes once halfway through.

9. Select "start/cancel" to stop cooking.

10. Serve hot.

NUTRITION: Calories: 195 Cal Total Fat: 8.8 g   Saturated Fat: 5.5 g   Cholesterol: 23 mg   Sodium: 110 mg   Total Carbs27.1 0 g   Fiber: 4.2 g   Sugar: 2.1 g   Protein: 3 g Potassium: 700 mg

36. Parmesan Brussels Sprout

Preparation time: 10 minutes

Cooking time: 10 minutes

Servings: 3

INGREDIENTS

- 1-pound brussels sprouts, trimmed and halved
- 1 tablespoon balsamic vinegar
- 1 tablespoon extra-virgin olive oil
- Salt and ground black pepper, as required
- ¼ cup whole-wheat breadcrumbs
- ¼ cup parmesan cheese, shredded

DIRECTIONS

1. Arrange the greased "inner basket" in air fryer toaster oven and press "preheat".
2. Select "start/cancel" to begin preheating.
3. When the unit beeps to show that it is preheated, arrange the brussels sprouts in "inner basket".
4. Insert the "inner basket" and select "air fry".
5. Set the temperature to 400 degrees f for 10 minutes.
6. Select "start/cancel" to begin cooking.
7. After 5 minutes, flip the Brussel sprouts and sprinkle with breadcrumbs, followed by the cheese.
8. Select "start/cancel" to stop cooking.

9. Serve hot.

NUTRITION: Calories: 170 Cal Total Fat: 7.5 g   Saturated Fat: 2.1 g   Cholesterol: 5 mg   Sodium: 267 mg   Total Carbs: 20.5 g   Fiber: 6.1 g   Sugar: 3.8 g   Protein: 8.9 g

CHAPTER 10:

EGGS & DAIRY

37. Baked Denver Omelet With Sausage

Preparation Time: 14 minutes

Servings: 5

INGREDIENTS

- 3 pork sausages, chopped
- 8 well-beaten eggs
- 1 ½ bell peppers, seeded and chopped
- 1 teaspoon smoked cayenne pepper
- 2 tablespoons Fontina cheese
- 1/2 teaspoon tarragon
- 1/2 teaspoon ground black pepper
- 1 teaspoon salt

DIRECTIONS

1. In a cast-iron skillet, sweat the bell peppers together with the chopped pork sausages until the peppers are fragrant and the sausage begins to release liquid.

2. Lightly grease the inside of a baking dish with pan spray.

3. Throw all of the above ingredients into the prepared baking dish, including the sautéed mixture; stir to combine.

4. Bake at 345 degrees F approximately 9 minutes. Serve right away with the salad of choice.

NUTRITION: 323 Calories; 18.6g Fat; 2.7g Carbs; 34.1g Protein; 1.4g Sugars; 0.4g Fiber

38. Baked Eggs With Beef And Tomato

Preparation Time: 20 minutes

Servings: 4

INGREDIENTS

- Non-stick cooking spray
- 1/2-pound leftover beef, coarsely chopped
- 2 garlic cloves, pressed
- 1 cup kale, torn into pieces and wilted
- 1 tomato, chopped
- 4 eggs, beaten
- 4 tablespoons heavy cream
- 1/2 teaspoon turmeric powder
- Salt and ground black pepper, to your liking
- 1/8 teaspoon ground allspice

DIRECTIONS

1. Spritz the inside of four ramekins with a cooking spray.
2. Divide all of the above ingredients among the prepared ramekins. Stir until everything is well combined.
3. Air-fry at 360 degrees F for 16 minutes; check with a wooden stick and return the eggs to the Air Fryer for a few more minutes as needed. Serve immediately.

NUTRITION: 236 Calories; 13.7g Fat; 4.1g Carbs; 23.8g Protein; 1.0g Sugars; 0.8g Fiber

39. Easy Frittata With Chicken Sausage

Preparation Time: 15 minutes

Servings: 2

INGREDIENTS

- 1 tablespoon olive oil

- 2 chicken sausages, sliced

- 4 eggs

- 1 garlic clove, minced

- 1/2 yellow onion, chopped

- Sea salt and ground black pepper, to taste

- 4 tablespoons Monterey-Jack cheese

- 1 tablespoon fresh parsley leaves, chopped

DIRECTIONS

1. Grease the sides and bottom of a baking pan with olive oil.

2. Add the sausages and cook in the preheated Air Fryer at 360 degrees F for 4 to 5 minutes.

3. In a mixing dish, whisk the eggs with garlic and onion. Season with salt and black pepper.

4. Pour the mixture over sausages. Top with cheese. Cook in the preheated Air Fryer at 360 degrees F for another 6 minutes.

5. Serve immediately with fresh parsley leaves. Bon appétit!

NUTRITION: 528 Calories; 42g Fat; 5.6g Carbs; 26.2g Protein; 2.6g Sugars; 0.8g Fiber

CHAPTER 11:

SIDE DISHES

40. Parsley Mushrooms

Preparation time: 10 minutes

Cooking time: 15 minutes

Servings: 4

INGREDIENTS

- 1-pound baby bella mushroom caps
- 1 teaspoon cumin, ground
- 1 tablespoon olive oil
- 2 teaspoons chili flakes, crushed
- 1 tablespoon parsley, chopped
- Salt and black pepper to the taste

DIRECTIONS

1. In your air fryer's basket, combine the mushroom caps with the cumin and the other ingredients, toss and cook at 380 degrees f for 15 minutes.
2. Divide between plates and serve as a side dish.

NUTRITION: Calories161, Fat 7, Fiber 1, Carbs 12, Protein6

41. <u>Paprika Corn And Kale</u>

Preparation time: 10 minutes

Cooking time: 15 minutes

Servings: 4

INGREDIENTS

- 2 cups fresh corn

- 1 cup baby kale

- Salt and black pepper to the taste

- 2 teaspoons olive oil

- Juice of 1 lime

- 1 teaspoon turmeric powder

- 2 teaspoons smoked paprika

DIRECTIONS

1. In your air fryer, combine the corn with the kale, oil and the other ingredients, toss and cook at 360 degrees f for 15 minutes.

2. Divide between plates and serve.

NUTRITION: Calories180, Fat 7, Fiber 2, Carbs 12, Protein6

CHAPTER 12:

SNACKS & APPETIZERS

42. Roasted Broccoli

Preparation time: 10 minutes

Cooking time: 15 minutes

Serving: 5

INGREDIENTS

- 1/8 tsp. Kosher salt

- 1/8 tsp. Black pepper

- 4 cups fresh broccoli (about a pound), trimmed

- 1 tsp. Olive oil

- 1/3 cup water

DIRECTION

1. Put broccoli in a bowl, add olive oil, salt and pepper then shake to mix

2. Put 1/4 cup of water to the base of the air fryer (under the basket in the actual basin) to avoid smoking while cooking

3. Place the broccoli to the air fryer basket and cook at 400f for 8 minutes

NUTRITION: 105 Calories 11g Fats 9g Protein

43. Banana Chips With Black Pepper

Preparation time: 10 minutes

Cooking time: 10 minutes

Servings: 4

INGREDIENTS

- 4 bananas, peeled and sliced in thin pieces
- A drizzle of olive oil
- A pinch of black pepper

DIRECTIONS

1. Put banana slices in your air fryer, drizzle the oil, season with pepper, toss to coat gently and cook at 360 degrees for 10 minutes.
2. Serve as a snack.
3. Enjoy!

NUTRITION: Calories100, Fat 7, Fiber 1, Carbs 20, Protein1

44. Cabbage Rolls

Preparation time: 10 minutes

Cooking time: 25 minutes

Servings: 8

INGREDIENTS

- 2 cups cabbage, chopped
- 2 yellow onions, chopped
- 1 carrot, chopped
- ½ red bell pepper, chopped
- 1-inch piece ginger, grated
- 8 garlic cloves, minced
- Salt and black pepper to the taste
- 1 teaspoon coconut aminos
- 2 tablespoons olive oil
- 10 vegan spring roll sheets
- Cooking spray
- 2 tablespoons corn flour mixed with 1 tablespoon water

DIRECTIONS

1. Heat up a pan with the oil over medium-high heat, add cabbage, onions, carrots, bell pepper, ginger, garlic, salt, pepper and aminos, stir, cook for 4 minutes and take off heat.
2. Cut each spring roll sheet and cut into 4 pieces.
3. Place 1 tablespoons veggie mix in one corner, roll and fold edges.

4. Repeat this with the rest of the rolls, place them in your air fryer's basket, grease them with cooking oil and cook at 360 degrees F for 10 minutes on each side.

5. Arrange on a platter and serve as an appetizer.

6. Enjoy!

NUTRITION: Calories150, Fat 3, Fiber 4, Carbs 7, Protein2

45. Tortilla Chips

Preparation time: 10 minutes

Cooking time: 4 minutes

Servings: 4

INGREDIENTS

- 8 corn tortillas, each cut into triangles

- Salt and black pepper to the taste

- 1 tablespoon olive oil

DIRECTIONS

1. Brush tortilla chips with the oil, place them in your air fryer's basket and cook for 4 minutes at 400 degrees F

2. Serve them with salt and pepper sprinkled all over.

3. Enjoy!

NUTRITION: Calories53, Fat 1, Fiber 1.5, Carbs 10, Protein2

46. Chickpeas With Cumin Snack

Preparation time: 10 minutes

Cooking time: 20 minutes

Servings: 4

INGREDIENTS

- 15 ounces canned chickpeas, drained
- ½ teaspoon cumin, ground
- 1 tablespoon olive oil
- 1 teaspoon smoked paprika
- Salt and black pepper to the taste

DIRECTIONS

1. In a bowl, mix chickpeas with oil, cumin, paprika, salt and pepper, toss to coat, place them in the fryer's basket, cook at 390 degrees F for 10 minutes and transfer to a bowl.

2. Serve as a snack

3. Enjoy!

NUTRITION: Calories140, Fat 1, Fiber 6, Carbs 20, Protein6

CHAPTER 13:

DESSERTS

47. Lentils And Dates Brownies With Honey And Banana Flavour

Preparation Time: 25 Minutes

Servings: 8

INGREDIENTS

- Canned lentils rinsed and drained- 28 ounces.
- Dates- 12
- Honey- 1 tbsp.
- Banana, peeled and chopped- 1
- Baking soda- ½ tsp.
- Almond butter- 4 tbsp.
- Cocoa powder- 2 tbsp.

DIRECTIONS

1. In a container of your food processor, add lentils, butter, banana, cocoa, baking soda, honey and blend it really well.

2. In it then add some dates, some more pulse before pouring it into a greased pan that fits your air dryer and spread evenly. Now bring it to fryer and let it bake for 15 minutes at 360 0F.

3. After it's done, take the brownies mix out of the oven and let it cool.

4. Lastly, cut them into pieces before arranging them on a platter to serve.

NUTRITION: Calories162, Fat 4, Fiber 2, Carbs 3, Protein4

48. Easy To Make Delicious Cheesecake

Preparation Time: 25 Minutes

Servings: 15

INGREDIENTS

- Cream cheese - 1 pound.
- Vanilla extract - ½ tsp.
- Eggs - 2
- Sugar - 4 tbsp.
- Graham crackers; crumbled - 1 cup.
- Butter - 2 tbsp.

DIRECTIONS

1. Take a bowl and in it mix crackers with butter. Now bring the crackers mix on the bottom of a lined cake pan and press it well. Cook it for 4 minutes in your air fryer at 350 degrees.

2. In the meantime, take another bowl and in it add some sugar, cream cheese, eggs, vanilla and whisk it well. Spread this filling over the crackers crust and cook it at 310 0for 15 minutes in your air fryer.

3. Leave the cake in your fridge for about 3 hours to cool down completely. Take it out and serve them in slices.

NUTRITION: Calories245, Fat 12, Fiber 1, Carbs 20, Protein3

49. <u>Ginger Flavoured Cheesecake</u>

Preparation Time: 2 hours and 30 Minutes

Servings: 6

INGREDIENTS

- Butter; melted - 2 tsps.
- Ginger cookies; crumbled - ½ cup.
- Cream cheese; soft - 16 ounces.
- Eggs - 2
- Sugar - ½ cup.
- Rum - 1 tsp.
- Vanilla extract - ½ tsp.
- Nutmeg; ground - ½ tsp.

DIRECTIONS

1. Take a pan and grease it well with butter.
2. Spread cookie crumbs on the bottom evenly.
3. Gather a mixer bowl to beat cream cheese with nutmeg, vanilla, rum and eggs.
4. Blend these ingredients together extremely well and spread it over cookie crumbs.
5. Set your air fryer at 340 0F for 20 minutes and put the pan into the fryer to cook.
6. Leave cheesecake to cool down completely and then put it in the fridge for 2 hours.

7. Slice into equal pieces and serve cold right away to enjoy it the most in the summer heat.

NUTRITION: Calories412, Fat 12, Fiber 6, Carbs 20, Protein6

50. Coffee Cheesecakes With Mascarpone Cheese On Top

Preparation Time: 30 Minutes

Servings: 6

INGREDIENTS

For the cheesecakes:

- Butter- 2 tbsp.

- Cream cheese- 8 ounces

- Coffee- 3 tbsp.

- Eggs- 3

- Sugar- 1/3 cup.

- Caramel syrup- 1 tbsp.

- For the frosting:

- Caramel syrup- 3 tbsp.

- Butter- 3 tbsp.

- Mascarpone cheese, soft- 8 ounces.

- Sugar- 2 tbsp.

DIRECTIONS

1. Take a blender and in it add cream cheese, eggs, 2 tbsp butter, coffee, 1 tbsp caramel syrup, ⅓ cup Sugar and mix it well. Now take a cupcake pan which fits in your air fryer and spoon the mixture in it before bringing it to the fryer and cook and let it bake for 20 minutes at 320 0F.

2. After it's done, take out the pan and leave it aside to cool down and then let it freeze in your fridge for another 3 hours.

3. In the meantime, take another bowl and mix 2 tbsp Sugar and mascarpone cheese and blend it well. After 3 hours take out the cake and ice it with this batter and serve them.

NUTRITION: Calories254, Fat 23, Fiber 0, Carbs 21, Protein5

CHAPTER 14:

MEAL PLAN FOR 21 DAYS

Days	Breakfast	Mains	Dessert
1.	Breakfast stuffed peppers	Air-fried chicken recipe	Chocolate mug cake
2.	Crispy breakfast potatoes	Air fried chinese pineapple pork	Apple pie
3.	Quick cheese omelet	Cauliflower and chickpea tacos	Banana brownies
4.	Tomato spinach frittata	Perfect air fryer salmon	Air fried biscuit donuts
5.	Roasted brussels sprouts & sweet potatoes	Air fryer buffalo cauliflower	Chocolate soufflé
6.	Roasted potato wedges	Air fryer Mexican-style stuffed chicken breast	Saucy fried bananas
7.	Breakfast egg bites	Lemon pepper shrimp	Crusty apple hand pies
8.	Grilled cheese sandwich	Air fried crumbed fish	Cream cheese wontons
9.	Nuts & seeds granola	Air fryer meatloaf	Cardamom spiced crumb cake
10.	Baked eggs	Air fryer shrimp a la bang	Peach cobbler
11.	Eggs in bread cups	Crumbed chicken tenderloins	Air fryer chocolate chip cookie
12.	Cream & cheddar omelet	Caribbean spiced chicken	Air fryer churro bites

13.	Bacon & kale frittata	Air fryer jalapeno popper hassel back chicken	Air fryer apple cider donuts
14.	Sausage with eggs	Air fryer steak & asparagus	Baked apple pudding
15.	Eggs with chicken	Lettuce salad with beef strips	Air baked lava cake
16.	Air fried mushroom frittata	Cayenne rib eye steak	Air fryer cheesecake egg rolls
17.	French toast from heaven!	Beef-chicken meatball casserole	Brazilian grilled pineapple
18.	Breakfast ham omelet	Juicy pork chops	Chocolate chunk walnut blondies
19.	Crunchy zucchini hash browns	Chicken goulash	Mexican brownies
20.	Crunchy hash browns	Chicken & turkey meatloaf	Chocolate chip cookie blondies
21.	Breakfast salmon patties	Turkey meatballs with dried dill	Blueberry lattice bars

CONCLUSION

I hope you enjoyed the recipes you found on this cookbook. I'm sure you've now found that Breville smart air fryer oven is a useful kitchen appliance that can help you prepare a variety of dishes for your family and friends. This appliance came as a relief for all the chefs and homemakers, who can now cook delicious crispy meals in no time: cook delicious breakfasts, juicy meat and poultry dishes, savory seafood, vegetables, and incredible desserts. Thanks to the newest technologies, all your meals are cooked quickly, and they are tasty and incredible. So, if you are planning to bring this kitchen marvel home, then don't wait around. Give it a try with the range of flavorsome recipes shared in this cookbook. I am sure that you will return to it again and again in search of tasty and favorite recipes.